APOLLO 11
LAUNCHES A NEW ERA

BY THOMAS K. ADAMSON

Published by The Child's World®
1980 Lookout Drive • Mankato, MN 56003-1705
800-599-READ • www.childsworld.com

Photographs ©: MSFC/NASA, cover, 1, 12, 16, 20, 25; NASA/dpa/picture-alliance/
Newscom, 6; JSC/NASA, 8, 15, 21, 22, 24, 28; KSC/NASA, 10, 11; Shutterstock Images,
17; Neil A. Armstrong/JSC/NASA, 18; JK/AP Images, 27

ISBN 9781503825178
LCCN 2017959668

Printed in the United States of America
PA02376

ABOUT THE AUTHOR

Thomas K. Adamson has written many space-related nonfiction books for
kids. He works at the Earth Resources Observation and Science (EROS)
Center, which collects satellite images of Earth. He enjoys reading, sports,
and spending time with his wife and two boys. He lives in Sioux Falls,
South Dakota.

TABLE OF CONTENTS

FAST FACTS

What was the relationship between the United States and the Soviet Union?

- From 1945 to 1991, the United States and the Soviet Union were in a **Cold War**. The two **superpowers** did not trust each other. They both built **atomic weapons** in a huge **arms race**. They also tried to become the first to accomplish major space exploration milestones in what was called the Space Race.

- Americans desperately wanted to beat the Soviet Union in the Space Race to show that they had better technology and had the ability to defend the country.

What were some of the first accomplishments in space?

- In October 1957, the Soviet Union launched *Sputnik*, the first artificial satellite, into **orbit**. Americans feared the Soviet Union could now spy on them or launch missiles from space.

- On January 31, 1958, the first U.S. satellite, *Explorer 1*, was launched into orbit.

TIMELINE

May 25, 1961: President John F. Kennedy addresses Congress and encourages the country to send humans to the moon by the end of the decade.

January 27, 1967: Astronauts Gus Grissom, Ed White, and Roger Chaffee die in a fire on Apollo 1.

July 16, 1969: Apollo 11 launches.

July 20, 1969: Astronauts Neil Armstrong and Edwin "Buzz" Aldrin land on the moon during the Apollo 11 mission. Armstrong becomes the first person to walk on the moon.

July 24, 1969: The Apollo 11 astronauts return safely to Earth.

December 11, 1972: The last Apollo mission to the moon, Apollo 17, lands on the moon.

December 14, 1972: Apollo 17 lifts off from the moon. This is the last time humans traveled to the moon.

Chapter 1

A MISSION TO THE MOON

President John F. Kennedy walked down a long aisle as members of Congress stood and clapped for him. Kennedy gripped a carefully prepared speech in his right hand. He smiled for the cameras. It was 1961 and Kennedy was a popular young president. But the United States was in a tense Cold War with the Soviet Union.

To beat the Soviets in the Space Race, Kennedy was ready to announce to Congress and the country a daring new idea.

Kennedy confidently stepped up to the podium. Members of Congress sat down and became silent. They waited for the president to speak. Kennedy's voice boomed through the room as he spoke into a microphone. Everyone listened intently as he described how America must take the lead in space achievements. He said, "I believe that this nation should commit itself to achieving the goal, before this decade is out, of landing a man on the moon and returning him safely to the Earth."[1]

Kennedy's decision to send astronauts to the moon was bold. Most people at the time thought going to the moon was an impossible dream. But Kennedy believed it was important to win the Space Race against the Soviet Union.

The National Aeronautics and Space Administration (NASA) organized a series of projects that would help to get astronauts on the moon. But the United States always seemed to be one step behind the Soviets. On February 3, 1966, the Soviet Union landed an unmanned spacecraft on the moon for the first time. It sent back the first pictures from the moon's surface.

▲ From left to right stand astronauts Ed
White, Gus Grissom, and Roger Chaffee.

The Soviets seemed close to achieving a manned mission
to the moon. But NASA was beginning to catch up in the
Space Race. NASA planned the first manned Apollo mission
for February 21, 1967. The Apollo missions focused on landing
astronauts on the moon and bringing them back safely to Earth.
Approximately one month before the first mission, astronauts
Gus Grissom, Ed White, and Roger Chaffee climbed into the
spacecraft to test its electrical systems. The astronauts sat tightly
side by side in their seats. In front of them was the control panel.

On the panel were many buttons and lights. Bundles of wires ran along the floor.

Grissom heard a crackling noise in his headset. The communications systems were not working well, and he became frustrated. He wondered how they could talk to Mission Control from the moon if they couldn't hear each other now. But the astronauts were confident they could solve the problems and get the job done.

Suddenly, the astronauts smelled smoke. They didn't have time to wonder where it came from before flames began racing up the wall inside the spacecraft. Bad wiring had sparked a fire. The astronauts felt the heat from bright flames. White yelled, "We've got a fire in the cockpit!"[2]

The astronauts rushed to open the **hatch**, but they could not open it in time. The temperature inside the spacecraft shot to 2,500 degrees Fahrenheit (1,400 degrees Celsius) in seconds. Chaffee cried, "We're burning up!"[3] In less than 30 seconds, the astronauts were dead.

The tragedy of Apollo 1 left people wondering if it was too difficult to get astronauts to the moon safely. NASA spent the next several months making the *Apollo* spacecraft safer. Engineers made better wiring that was less likely to become damaged. They designed a hatch that was easier to open.

▲ Today, people remember the Apollo 1 tragedy.

NASA continued working on *Apollo* test flights and learned a lot about how to land a spacecraft on the moon. All of these achievements built upon one another. Then came the Apollo 11 mission in 1969, which accomplished Kennedy's dream of landing people on the moon.

In 2017, NASA opened an Apollo 1 exhibit at the Kennedy ▶ Space Center in Florida.

Chapter 2

MOON LANDING

On July 16, 1969, astronauts Neil Armstrong, Michael Collins, and Edwin "Buzz" Aldrin walked across a high platform to the top of the rocket that would take them into space. They were already sealed inside their spacesuits. It was a hot, humid summer day at Kennedy Space Center in Florida. A clear sky made for great conditions for a launch.

The three men had spent several months preparing for their
mission to land on the moon. They hoped all that planning
would pay off. NASA workers helped them climb into the small
spacecraft. They closed the hatch to seal them in. Strapped
tightly in their seats, the three astronauts listened to the
countdown in their headsets. Lights, switches, and gauges lined
the walls. They were relieved to see that everything was running
perfectly. A huge roar erupted beneath them as they prepared
for takeoff. The cabin shook violently, but the astronauts
remained calm. This was not their first trip into space.

In just 12 minutes, they entered Earth's orbit. They fired one
more engine that sent them on a course toward the moon. It
took three days to get there. On July 19, they were finally able
to see the moon up close out of their small windows. Armstrong
and Aldrin felt excited about landing on the moon. But first, they
needed a good night's sleep.

On July 20, Armstrong and Aldrin moved into the **lunar
module** named *Eagle*. The lunar module was built to do one
thing: land on the moon. Collins stayed in the command module,
called *Columbia*. This part of the spacecraft stayed in orbit
around the moon. It held the fuel to bring them back to Earth.

As *Eagle* undocked from *Columbia* to travel to the moon's surface, Armstrong smiled to himself and said, "The *Eagle* has wings."[4]

As *Eagle* flew down toward the moon, a series of computer alarms went off. A light flashed in front of Aldrin: "Program Alarm." He pressed a button. The next flash said "1202." This was an alarm that never came up in **simulations**. The alarm meant the computer was doing too many calculations and couldn't keep up. It could stop the landing attempt.

However, flight controllers quickly realized that if the alarm was not continuous, the computer was okay and they could go ahead with the landing. Armstrong began looking for a landing site. He looked out the window and didn't like what he saw. The computer was about to put them down in a field of boulders. Some boulders were the size of small cars. Armstrong took control of *Eagle*. Next to the boulders there was a large **crater**. Armstrong knew it wasn't safe to land too close to a crater, and certainly not inside one. *Eagle* could land at an angle and then not be able to lift off. Armstrong said, "I gotta get farther over here."[5] He calmly flew *Eagle* over the crater. There was only 60 seconds of fuel left.

The rocket used to take Apollo 11 to the moon was ▶ 636 feet (194 m) tall.

▲ When *Eagle* landed, it only had 30 seconds of fuel remaining.

Aldrin watched the data on his computer, which told them *Eagle*'s speed and distance from the surface. They were gradually getting closer. Finally, Aldrin saw what he was waiting for and exclaimed, "Contact light!"[6] The lander's feet had touched the surface! Armstrong shut off the engine. The two men smiled at each other and shook hands. Then, Armstrong spoke to Mission Control in Houston, Texas, "The *Eagle* has landed."[7]

At Mission Control, the room erupted in cheers. Astronaut Charlie Duke was the only one at Mission Control who could talk to the astronauts. He replied, "We copy you on the ground.

You got a bunch of guys about to turn blue. We're breathing again. Thanks a lot."[8] On *Eagle*, Armstrong and Aldrin felt their hearts race as they prepared to step onto the moon's surface.

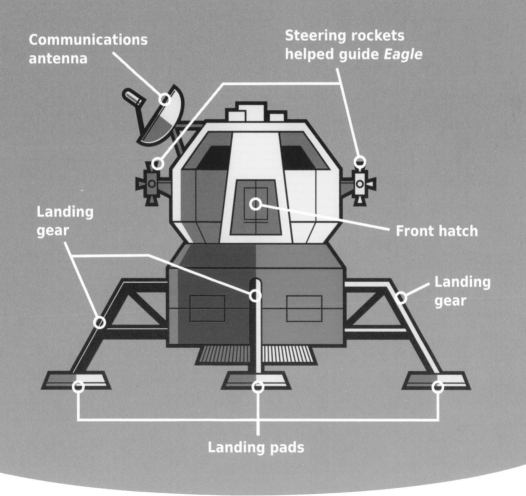

LUNAR MODULE *EAGLE*

Communications antenna

Steering rockets helped guide *Eagle*

Landing gear

Front hatch

Landing gear

Landing pads

Chapter 3

EXPLORATION

Armstrong and Aldrin helped each other put on their bulky backpacks with oxygen tanks. There wasn't much room inside *Eagle*, and they tried not to bump any of the switches on the walls. Once they were ready, the astronauts took deep breaths. Aldrin guided Armstrong through the hatch. NASA knew it was important to let everyone see this moment. Before he climbed down the ladder, Armstrong paused.

He turned on a TV camera on the side of *Eagle*. In stores, restaurants, and homes around the world, people were glued to their TVs. An estimated 600 million people watched Armstrong move carefully down the ladder and onto the moon. It was the largest audience for any event in history at the time.

Now at the bottom of the ladder, Armstrong stepped carefully onto the moon's dusty surface. He said, "That's one small step for man, one giant leap for mankind."[9] No one was sure how difficult it would be to walk on the moon. Once there, Armstrong thought it was no trouble at all. The gravity on the moon is lower than Earth's, and even with Armstrong's bulky suit and backpack, he weighed only 60 pounds (27 kg).

Aldrin climbed down the ladder after Armstrong. As he reached the surface, he stood in awe of the scene. The gray surface of the moon contrasted with the dark black sky. Aldrin then looked in wonder at the ground. He kicked up the moon dust, and it landed in a perfect arc. He marveled at the prints his boots left on the moon's surface. Later, Aldrin described what it was like to be there, "It's pretty much without color. It's a very white, chalky gray."[10]

Both Aldrin and Armstrong were amazed by the experience, but they had work to do. They set up some science experiments.

One experiment used a device that would collect solar wind
samples. They also set up an instrument that would record
moonquakes. And they picked up moon rocks and took lots
of pictures.

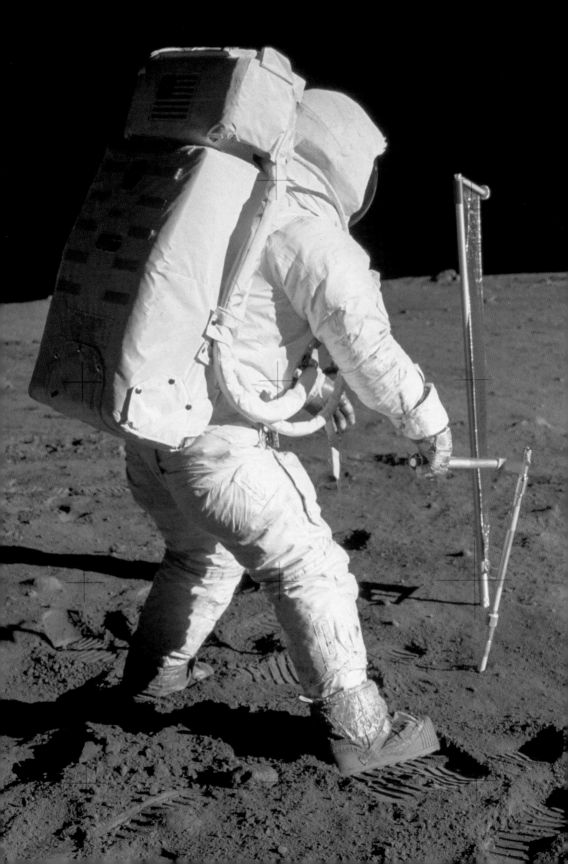

After approximately two hours, Mission Control said their moonwalk was extended for another 15 minutes. Armstrong bolted off at a hopping run toward the crater he had flown over before landing. It was tempting to climb down and get some valuable rock samples, but Armstrong knew it would be too dangerous. He settled for taking pictures of the crater and of *Eagle*. He headed back to *Eagle*, satisfied with the few minutes of real exploring.

Back inside, the astronauts found that the moon dust stuck to everything. They also noticed a strange odor. It reminded them of wet ashes, and they wondered if that was how the moon smelled. They then rested for a few hours before getting ready to lift off from the moon.

As they prepared the computer for liftoff, Aldrin noticed a black piece of plastic lying on the floor. He picked it up and discovered it was a switch from one of the control panels. He believed it must have broken off when they were putting on their bulky backpacks. The switch belonged to the circuit breaker that armed the engine. They really needed that switch!

Thinking fast, Aldrin grabbed a felt-tip pen. He crammed it into the space where the switch had broken off, and it worked. The engine ignited and *Eagle* lifted off the moon's surface.

◀ Collins helped *Eagle* dock on the command module once it returned from the moon.

Chapter 4

INFLUENCE OF APOLLO 11

Just as there was only one chance at the landing, the astronauts only had one shot at reentering Earth's **atmosphere**. If they entered the atmosphere too fast, the spacecraft would catch fire and burn up. If they entered too slowly, they would bounce off the atmosphere and back into space with no option to try again.

◄ The Apollo 11 astronauts were recovered 934 miles (1,503 km) southwest of Hawaii.

After the spacecraft entered Earth's atmosphere, three large orange-and-white-striped parachutes flew open to slow down the descent. Still, the spacecraft slammed into the Pacific Ocean and jolted the three men. Helicopters from the navy ship USS *Hornet* flew to get the astronauts.

▲ Armstrong (middle), Collins, and Aldrin were placed in isolation once arriving on the *Hornet*.

A navy swimmer jumped from the helicopter into the ocean. He inflated a rubber raft. Then, he swam to the spacecraft, opened the hatch, and peered inside. The exhausted astronauts looked dirty and unshaven. But they were safe. The navy diver dropped three one-piece suits inside. Armstrong, Aldrin, and Collins struggled to put these suits on in the tiny spacecraft. They were required to wear these in case they had any moon germs.

The navy swimmer then helped the astronauts onto the raft. The high waves rocked the spacecraft and the raft, making their work difficult. Then, the astronauts were hoisted up to the helicopter and flown to the *Hornet*. Once they were on the ship, the astronauts waved at the navy sailors who greeted them. The astronauts' legs felt a little wobbly. It would take some time for them to get used to Earth's gravity.

Armstrong, Aldrin, and Collins were heroes. People all over the world wanted to see them. A huge crowd gathered in New York City for a parade in their honor. The astronauts felt overwhelmed by all the attention. Four million people lined the streets and watched out of windows to cheer for them. Confetti and streamers covered them and the convertibles in which they rode.

The Apollo 11 astronauts were celebrated in New York City on ▶ August 13, 1969.

▲ The Apollo 11 astronauts took pictures of Earth during the space mission.

They attended many more parades all over the United States. They also traveled around the world so people could hear more about their incredible journey.

Pictures that the astronauts took were shown to the public. People began to see Earth as a fragile and unique place. They started new movements to work on protecting Earth.

Americans embraced the Apollo 11 mission as part of their culture. Many people who watched the astronauts step onto the moon thought they would never look at the moon the same way again. Others became convinced that because the United States had put humans on the moon, the country could do anything. Armstrong addressed Congress in 1969 and said, "Responding to challenge is one of democracy's great strengths. Our successes in space lead us to hope that this strength can be used in the next decade in the solution of many of our planet's problems."[11]

THINK ABOUT IT

- How does having a clear goal, such as landing on the moon within a specific time frame, help get something big accomplished?
- If it weren't for the Space Race with the Soviet Union, would humans have ever landed on the moon? Explain your reasoning.
- Humans haven't been to the moon since 1972. Why do you think this is?

GLOSSARY

arms race (ARMS RAYSS): An arms race is when countries compete with one another to build more bombs and missiles. The United States and the Soviet Union were in an arms race during the Cold War.

atmosphere (AT-muhss-feer): Atmosphere is the mixture of gases surrounding a planet. The Apollo 11 crew entered Earth's atmosphere when they returned from the moon.

atomic weapons (uh-TOM-ik WEP-uhns): Atomic weapons are bombs that explode with great energy and force. The United States and the Soviet Union were building atomic weapons during the Cold War.

Cold War (KOHLD WOR): A Cold War occurs when two countries are politically hostile toward one another. The United States and Soviet Union were in a Cold War.

crater (KRAY-tur): A crater is a hole in the ground caused by something smashing into it. Neil Armstrong saw a crater on the moon.

hatch (HACH): A hatch is a small door on a spacecraft that covers an opening in a wall. The astronauts left the lunar module through a hatch.

lunar module (LOO-nur MOJ-ool): A lunar module is a space vehicle used to transport astronauts to the moon from the command module. Two of the Apollo 11 astronauts rode a lunar module called *Eagle*.

orbit (OR-bit): An orbit is the path followed by a planet, moon, or other object as it goes around a planet, moon, or the sun. The Apollo 11 astronauts went into orbit around the moon before landing on it.

simulations (sim-yuh-LAY-shuhns): Simulations are trial runs to test out a real event. Astronauts and Mission Control ran many simulations of the moon landing before the Apollo 11 mission.

superpowers (SOO-pur-pow-urs): Superpowers are countries that are large and have a big influence on the rest of the world. The United States and the Soviet Union were the world's two superpowers during the Cold War.

SOURCE NOTES

1. "Excerpt from an Address before a Joint Session of Congress, 25 May 1961." *John F. Kennedy Presidential Library and Museum*. John F. Kennedy Presidential Library and Museum, 25 May 1961. Web. 31 Oct. 2017.

2. Dan Parry. *Moonshot: The Inside Story of Mankind's Greatest Adventure.* London, England: Ebury Press, 2009. Print. 83.

3. Ibid. 84.

4. "Phase 5: Descent to the Moon." *Spacelog Apollo 11.* Spacelog, n.d. Web. 31 Oct. 2017.

5. Andrew Chaikin. *A Man on the Moon: The Voyages of the Apollo Astronauts.* New York, NY: Viking, 1994. Print. 198.

6. Craig Nelson. *Rocket Men: The Epic Story of the First Men on the Moon.* New York, NY: Viking, 2009. Print. 258.

7. "Apollo 11 Lunar Surface Journal." *NASA.* NASA, n.d. Web. 31 Oct. 2017.

8. Ibid.

9. Ibid.

10. Craig Nelson. *Rocket Men: The Epic Story of the First Men on the Moon.* New York, NY: Viking, 2009. Print. 267.

11. Ibid.

TO LEARN MORE

Books

Green, Carl R. *Walking on the Moon: The Amazing Apollo 11 Mission.* Berkeley Heights, NJ: Enslow, 2013.

Nagelhout, Ryan. *The First Moon Walk.* New York, NY: Gareth Stevens, 2015.

Thimmesh, Catherine. *Team Moon: How 400,000 People Landed Apollo 11 on the Moon.* Boston, MA: Houghton Mifflin Harcourt, 2015.

Web Sites

Visit our Web site for links about Apollo 11: childsworld.com/links

Note to Parents, Teachers, and Librarians: We routinely verify our Web links to make sure they are safe and active sites. So encourage your readers to check them out!

INDEX